SPOTLIGHT ON SOCIAL AND EMOTIONAL LEARNING

KEEPING CALM AND FOCUSED

STRESS MANAGEMENT

THERESA EMMINIZER

PowerKiDS press.

NEW YORK

Published in 2020 by The Rosen Publishing Group, Inc.
29 East 21st Street, New York, NY 10010

Editor: Elizabeth Krajnik
Designer: Michael Flynn

Photo Credits: Cover, p. 21 FatCamera/E+/Getty Images; cover, pp. 1, 3–8, 10–12, 14, 16, 18–20, 22–24 (background) TairA/Shutterstock.com; p. 4 Sabphoto/Shutterstock.com; p. 5 Bettmann/Getty Images; p. 6 Aaron Amat/Getty Images; p. 7 Zivica Kerkez/Shutterstock.com; p. 9 Letizia Le Fur/ONOKY/Getty Images; p. 10 Alena Ozerova/Shutterstock.com; p. 11 Diego Cervo/Shutterstock.com; p. 13 Lapina/Shutterstock.com; p. 14 Ryzhkov Photography/Shutterstock.com; p. 15 Dreams Come True/Shutterstock.com; p. 17 HOANG DINH NAM/AFP/Getty Images; p. 18 Courtesy of the Library of Congress; p. 19 Skolkokrasok/Shutterstock.com; p. 22 V.S.Anandhakrishna/Shutterstock.com.

Cataloging-in-Publication Data

Names: Emminizer, Theresa.
Title: Keeping calm and focused: stress management / Theresa Emminizer.
Description: New York : PowerKids Press, 2020. | Series: Spotlight on social and emotional learning | Includes glossary and index.
Identifiers: ISBN 9781725302068 (pbk.) | ISBN 9781725302259 (library bound) | ISBN 9781725302167 (6pack)
Subjects: LCSH: Stress management--Juvenile literature. | Stress management for teenagers--Juvenile literature. | Stress management for children--Juvenile literature. | Stress in adolescence--Juvenile literature. | Stress in children--Juvenile literature.
Classification: LCC RA785.E46 2020 | DDC 155.9'042--dc23

Manufactured in the United States of America

CPSIA Compliance Information: Batch #CSPK19. For further information contact Rosen Publishing, New York, New York at 1-800-237-9932.

CONTENTS

CHAPTER ONE

WHAT IS STRESS?

Stress is a state of tension, or a feeling of nervousness that makes it hard to relax. It's also a state of worry caused by problems or demands, things that require your attention, in your life. Stress affects your feelings, mind, and body. Sometimes it can give you a stomachache, make you feel upset, and make it hard for you to sleep. Stress is usually your body's way of telling you that you're overwhelmed, or have too many things to deal with, and something needs to change.

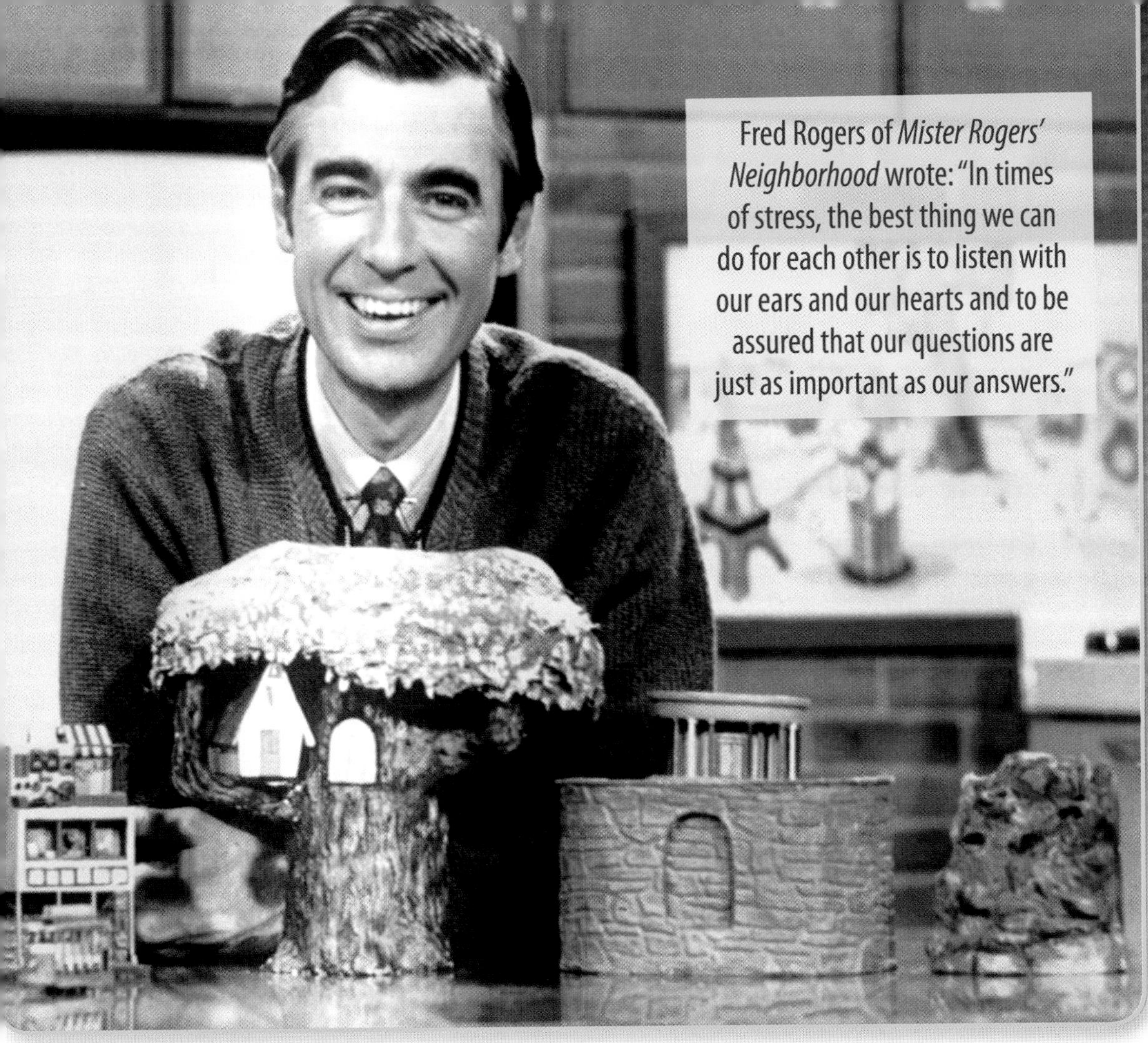

Fred Rogers of *Mister Rogers' Neighborhood* wrote: "In times of stress, the best thing we can do for each other is to listen with our ears and our hearts and to be assured that our questions are just as important as our answers."

Stress is a normal part of life. But if we don't learn to cope, or deal, with it in a healthy way, stress can make it hard to think clearly, feel well, and enjoy life. It's impossible to cure stress or make it go away completely. However, you can learn positive ways to cope with it that will make you feel more in control.

CHAPTER TWO

IDENTIFY YOUR STRESSORS

The first step to coping with stress is to figure out what's causing it. Take a moment to reflect on what's going on in your life. Is there something going on that's making you feel uncomfortable or unhappy? Can you identify a situation in which you feel worried or **frustrated**?

HOMEWORK

VIOLIN LESSONS

SWIM PRACTICE

PEER PRESSURE

STRESSORS

FAMILY FIGHT

LOST LIBRARY BOOK

IMPORTANT TEST

SLEEPOVERS

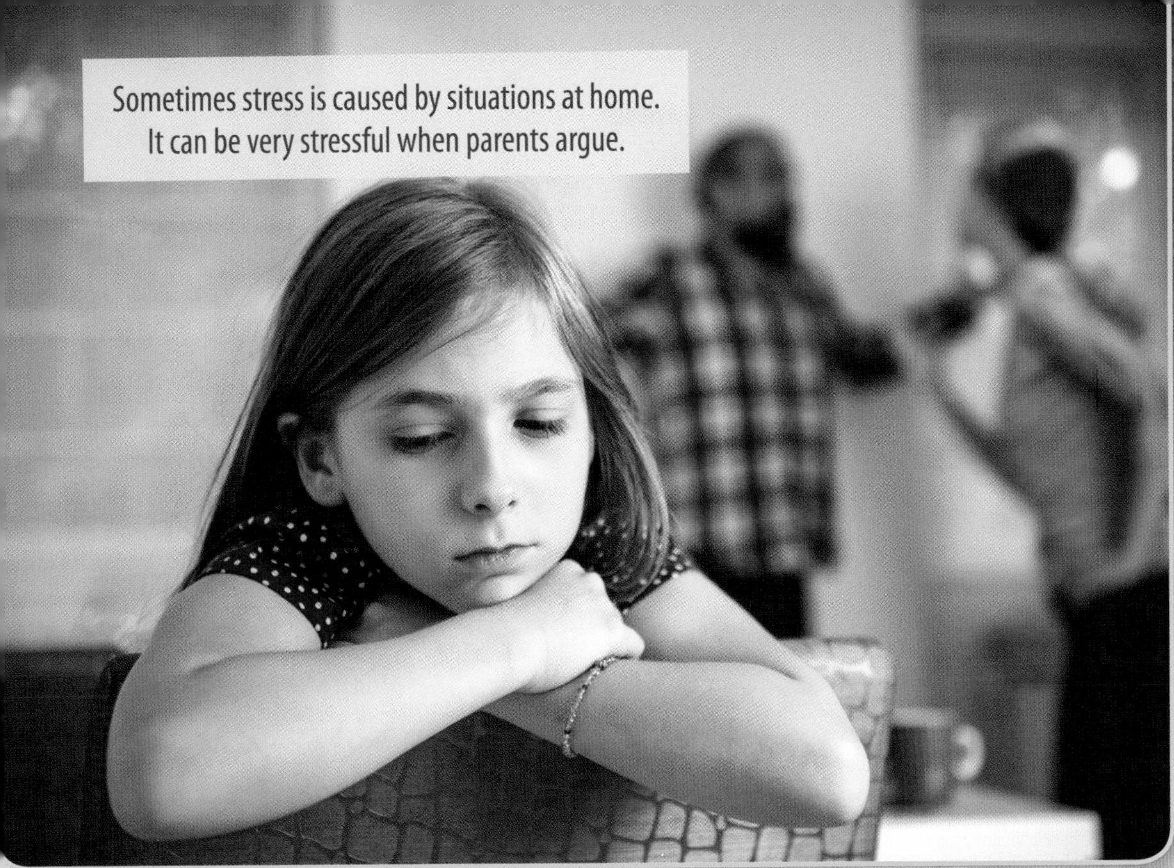

Sometimes stress is caused by situations at home. It can be very stressful when parents argue.

Sometimes stressors, or things that cause stress, are temporary. This means they don't last a very long time or forever. You might be worried about a big test coming up. With temporary stressors, the feelings of discomfort usually go away after the stressful event is over. Other stressors are chronic, or continue for a long time or return often. Are you trying to juggle schoolwork, swim practice, violin lessons, and sleepovers with friends? You might have too much going on! When you're constantly active, your mind and body don't have time to relax.

CHAPTER THREE

ASK FOR HELP

You might not be able to figure out what's causing your stress. Maybe you aren't worrying about a single event or feeling too busy. That's OK! Sometimes just going about our daily lives is enough to make us feel stressed.

No matter what's causing your stress, the most helpful thing to do is tell someone about it. The simple act of sharing your feelings can help relieve some of the pressure that's been building up inside you. When you talk about your feelings, you start to understand them better. Talk to someone who makes you feel comfortable and safe. It could be a friend, a parent, a teacher, or a **counselor**. It might be hard, but there's no reason to feel upset. Everyone experiences stress. Those people might have ideas about how to handle it.

You're not alone! Stress is something that all people deal with. Talking about it can help.

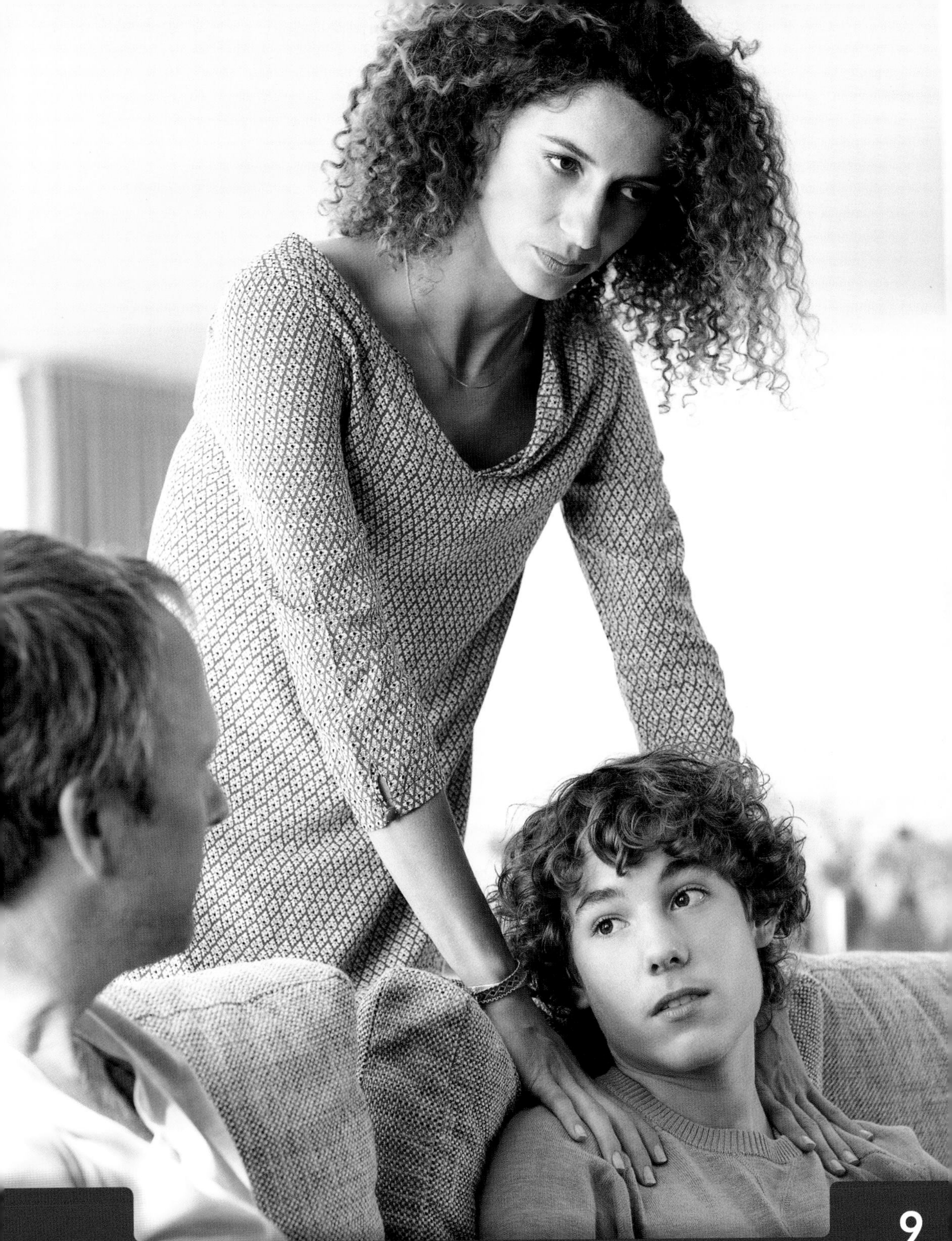

CHAPTER FOUR

TAKE A BREAK

If you're able to identify the situations that cause you to feel stressed, make an effort to avoid or remove yourself from them. Maybe watching the news makes you feel upset about what's going on in the world around you. Take a break! Turn off the TV or go into another room where you don't have to watch or listen to it.

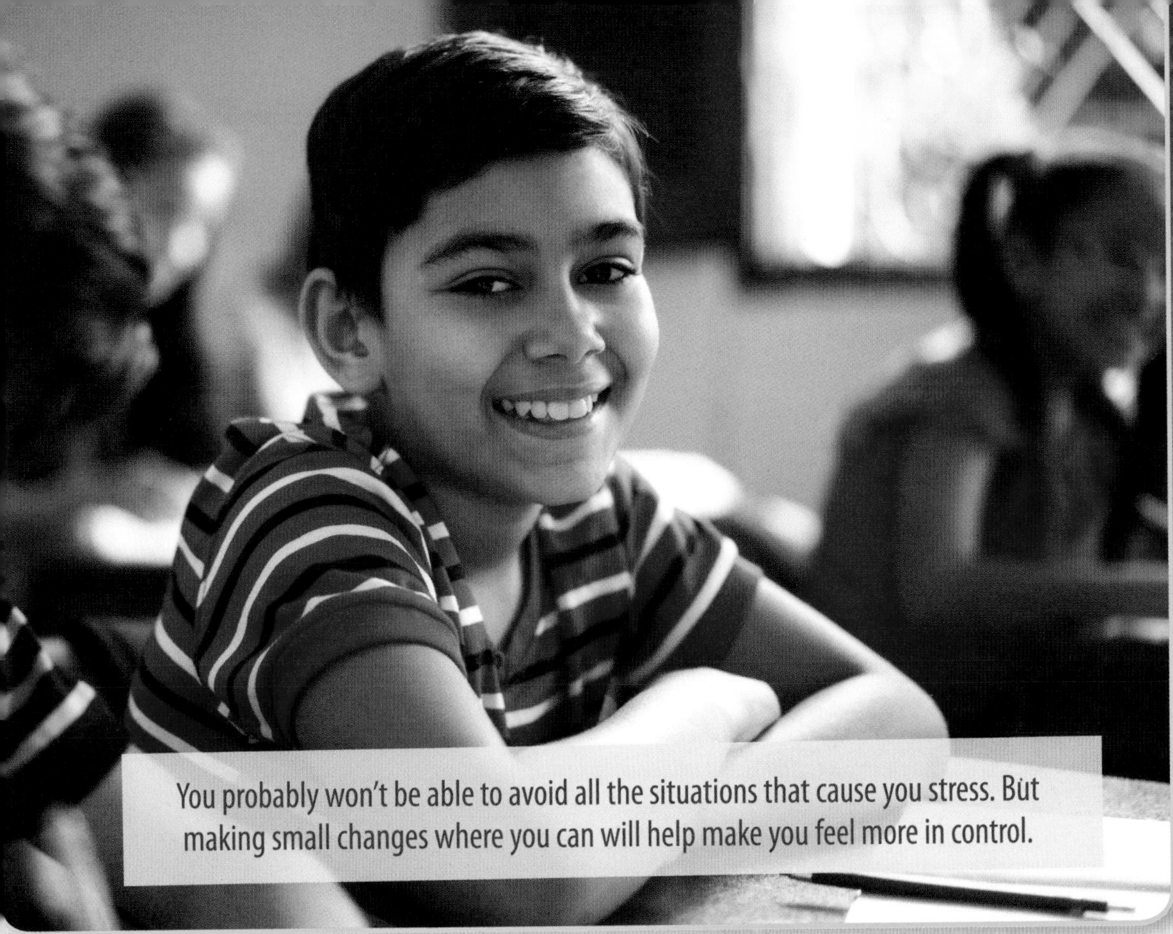

You probably won't be able to avoid all the situations that cause you stress. But making small changes where you can will help make you feel more in control.

Maybe you feel **competitive** or frustrated when you see or hear that one of your classmates is getting better grades than you. Take a break! Stay out of conversations about grades if you can. If you feel overbooked, see if you can cut back on some of your activities. If you have a friend who has a bad **attitude** and always complains, stay away from them for a while! Try to distance yourself from the people, situations, and things that make you feel upset.

CHAPTER FIVE

LISTEN TO YOUR BODY

You won't be able to take a break from everything that causes you stress. Maybe you hate going to the doctor's office and feel very worried and uncomfortable every time you have to go in for a checkup. Luckily, there are exercises that can help you cope when you're faced with an unavoidable stressor.

When you're in a stressful situation, it can be hard to **function** normally. Stress can make your head ache or make you feel sick to your stomach. **Focus** on your body and listen to its signals. Do you feel light-headed? Plant your feet firmly on the ground. Sometimes when we're nervous, we may breathe very quickly and deeply. Breathe in slowly and deeply through your nose. Breathe out slowly through your mouth. Breathing slowly and deeply will help you take in the right amount of air and calm you down.

> You can do breathing exercises anywhere, anytime. It's likely that no one will even know you're doing them!

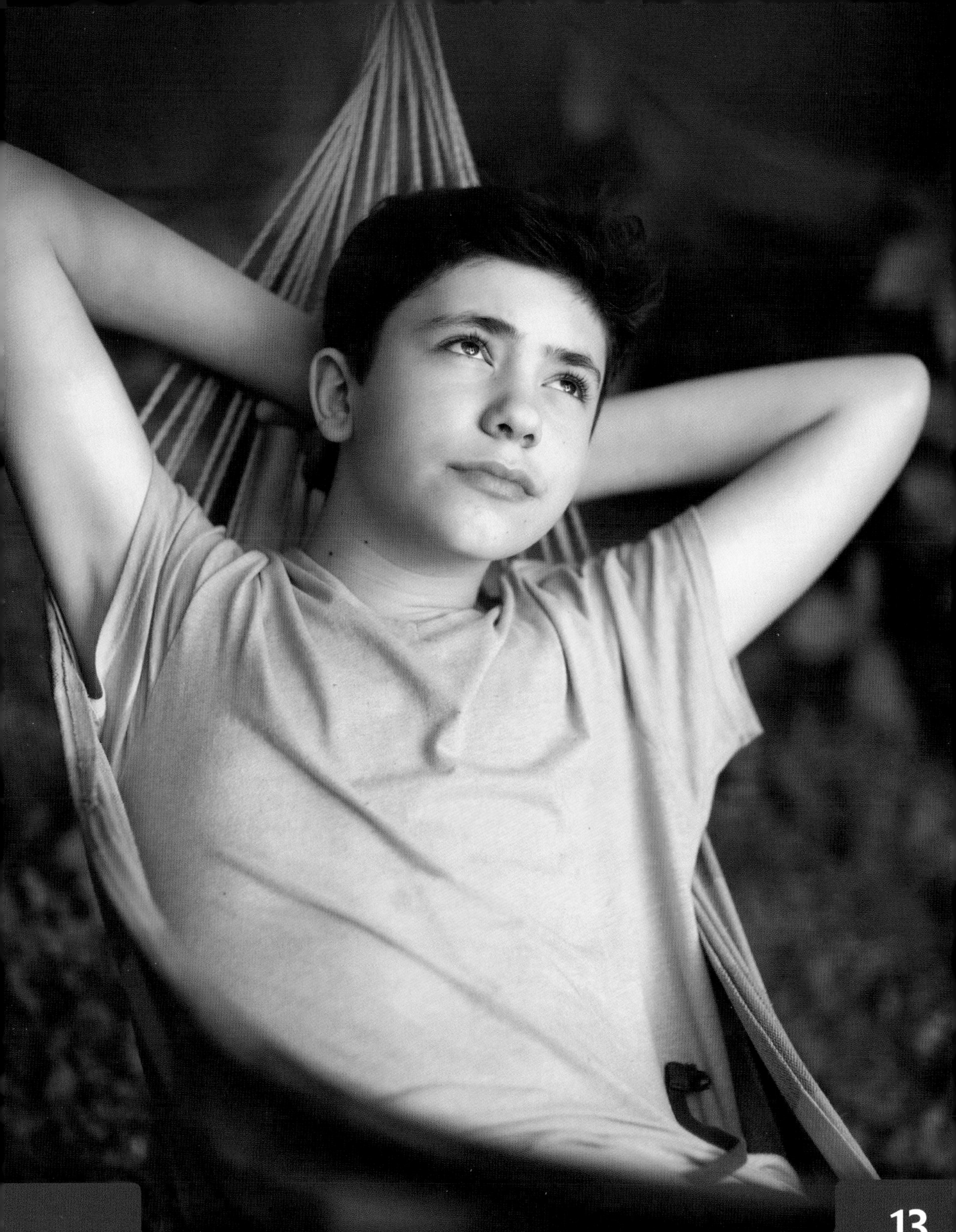

CHAPTER SIX

CREATE HEALTHY ROUTINES

Your body, mind, and feelings are all interconnected. When one is affected, the others are too. Maybe your stress is making it hard for you to fall asleep at night. When you lie in bed, your thoughts spin in a circle as you go over all the worries and fears you have on your mind. The next day, you wake up cranky and tired because you didn't get the rest you needed, and you feel even more stressed than the day before!

When you're stressed, it's important to create healthy **routines** and stick to them. You're much more capable of dealing with stress when you eat regularly, get enough sleep, and do some sort of exercise. This doesn't mean you should try to force yourself to sleep when you can't. Try writing down your thoughts in a journal, listening to gentle music, or **meditating**.

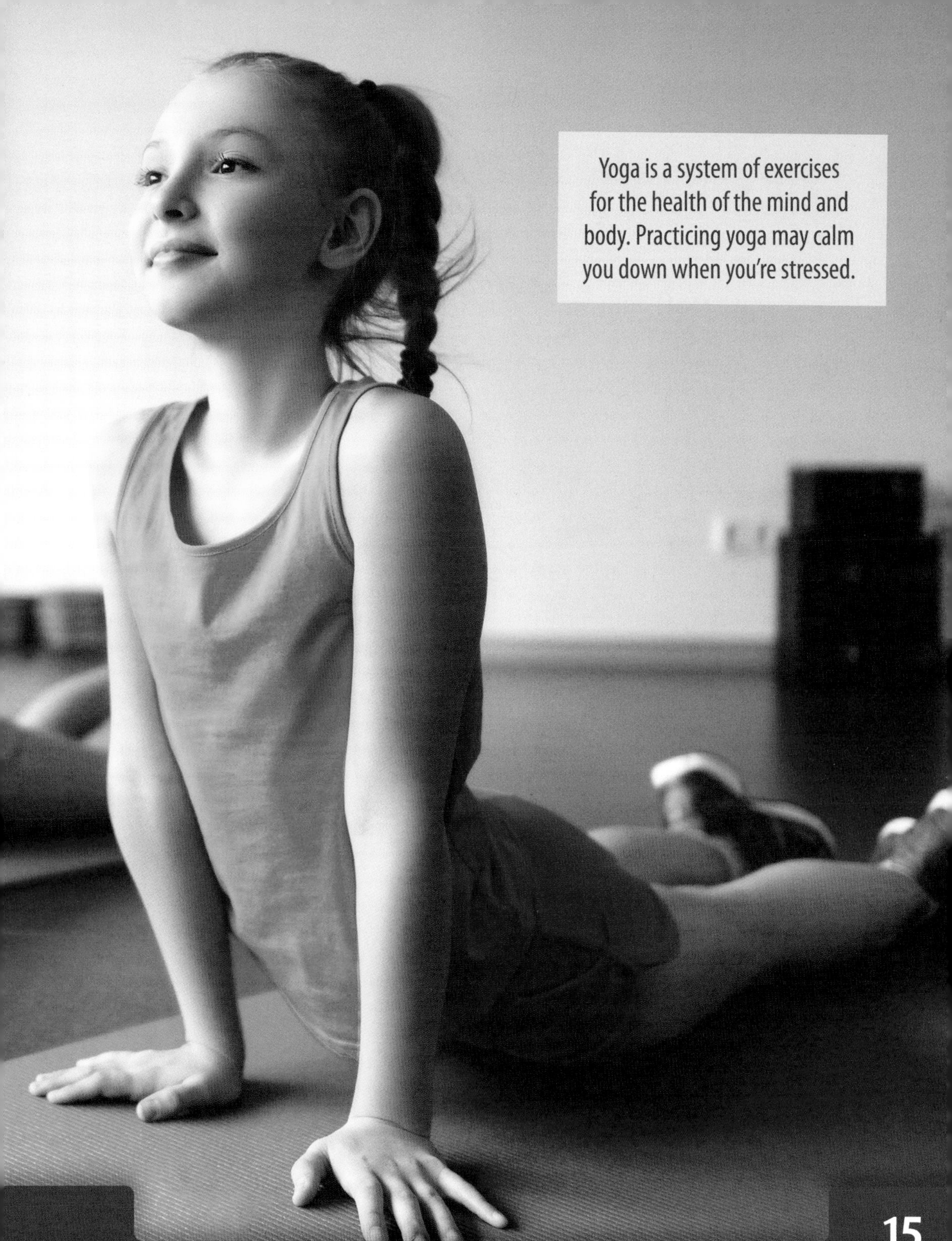

Yoga is a system of exercises for the health of the mind and body. Practicing yoga may calm you down when you're stressed.

CHAPTER SEVEN

THINK WITHOUT JUDGMENT

Sometimes stress can lead to catastrophic thinking. Catastrophic thinking is being obsessed about, or being hung up on, the worst possible **scenarios** and outcomes. For example, if you're nervous about going on a field trip, you might imagine that the bus is going to crash on the way there. This kind of thinking is **irrational** and allowing it to affect your behavior is unhealthy.

Catastrophic thoughts are scary and can be hard to stop. But it's important to remind yourself that thoughts are just thoughts. They aren't facts or truths. Try not to feel bad about them! Thoughts come and go. When you have a catastrophic thought, observe it without judgment. Don't be afraid of it. **Acknowledge** the thought and then simply let it go. When you observe your thoughts without judgment, you are able to free yourself from them.

Thich Nhat Hanh, pictured here, is a **Buddhist** monk. He wrote: "When a feeling or thought arises, your **intention** should not be to chase it away."

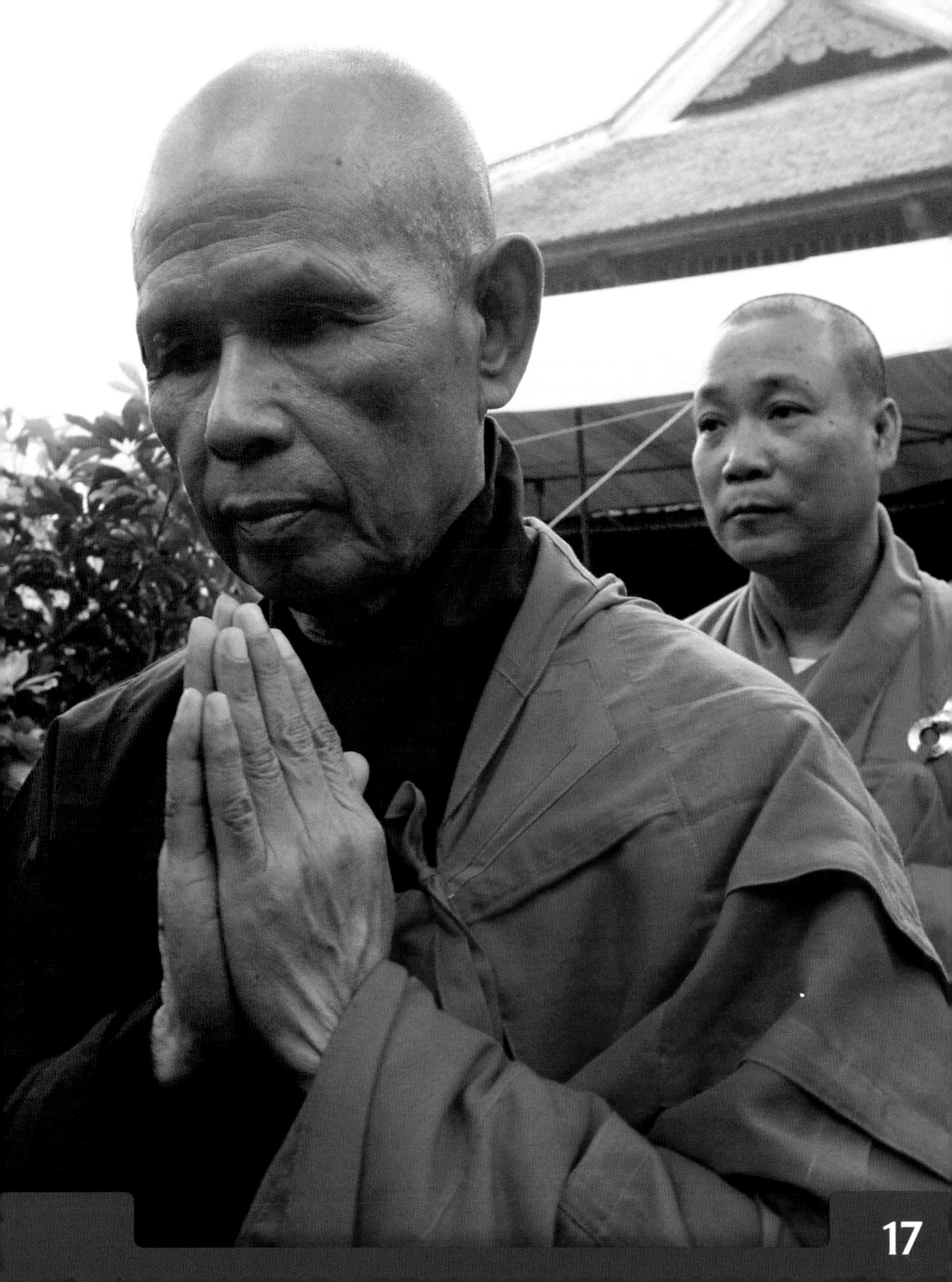

CHAPTER EIGHT

CREATE A MANTRA

When you're stressed, you might feel like it will last forever. It's important to remember that, like our thoughts, our feelings come and go. Stress isn't a permanent, or long-lasting, condition. When times get difficult, or hard to deal with, you may be able to work through stress by creating a mantra.

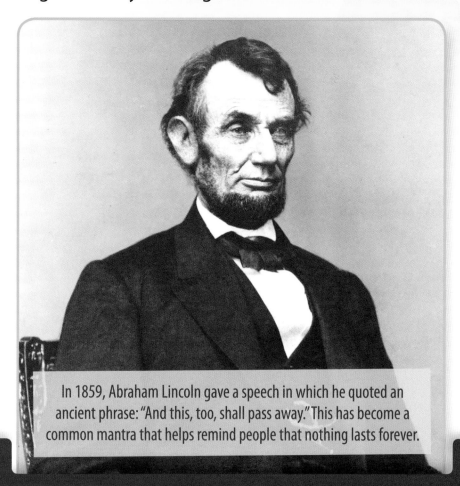

In 1859, Abraham Lincoln gave a speech in which he quoted an ancient phrase: "And this, too, shall pass away." This has become a common mantra that helps remind people that nothing lasts forever.

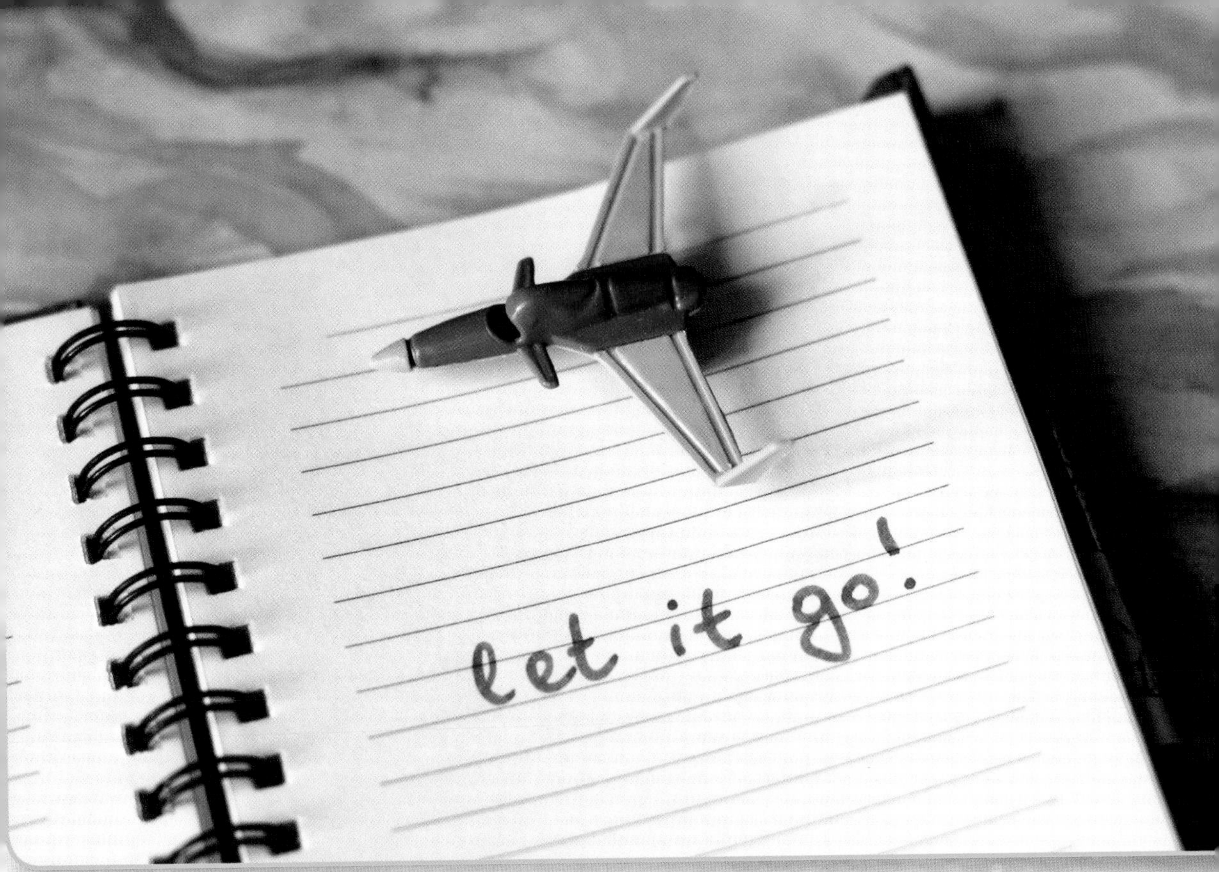
let it go!

A mantra is a statement that you repeat to yourself. For example, when you feel overwhelmed by stress, you could look in the mirror and say, "Peace is within me." Another popular mantra is, "Let it go."

There is no one perfect mantra. Choose a phrase that comforts you and makes you feel strong. You might feel silly at first, but you'll soon find that your mantra can help reassure you when you feel upset. You can say your mantra out loud or repeat it silently in your head when you're in public.

CHAPTER NINE

BE PRESENT

Stress isn't fun, and you'll likely experience it many times throughout your life. Although you can't avoid stress, **developing** calmness can help you cope with it. How do you develop calmness? One way to develop calmness is by practicing being present.

When you're stressed, it can feel like there aren't enough hours in the day. Because you're worried about the future, you rush through each moment and fail to enjoy it because you're focused on what's coming next. Instead of worrying about the future, make an effort to be present. Focus only on what's going on right now.

You only have the power to control what you do in the present. When you focus on the present, you can let go of your stress about the future and pay attention to the things you're able to do right now.

If you take your day one thing at a time, you will feel calmer and less stressed.

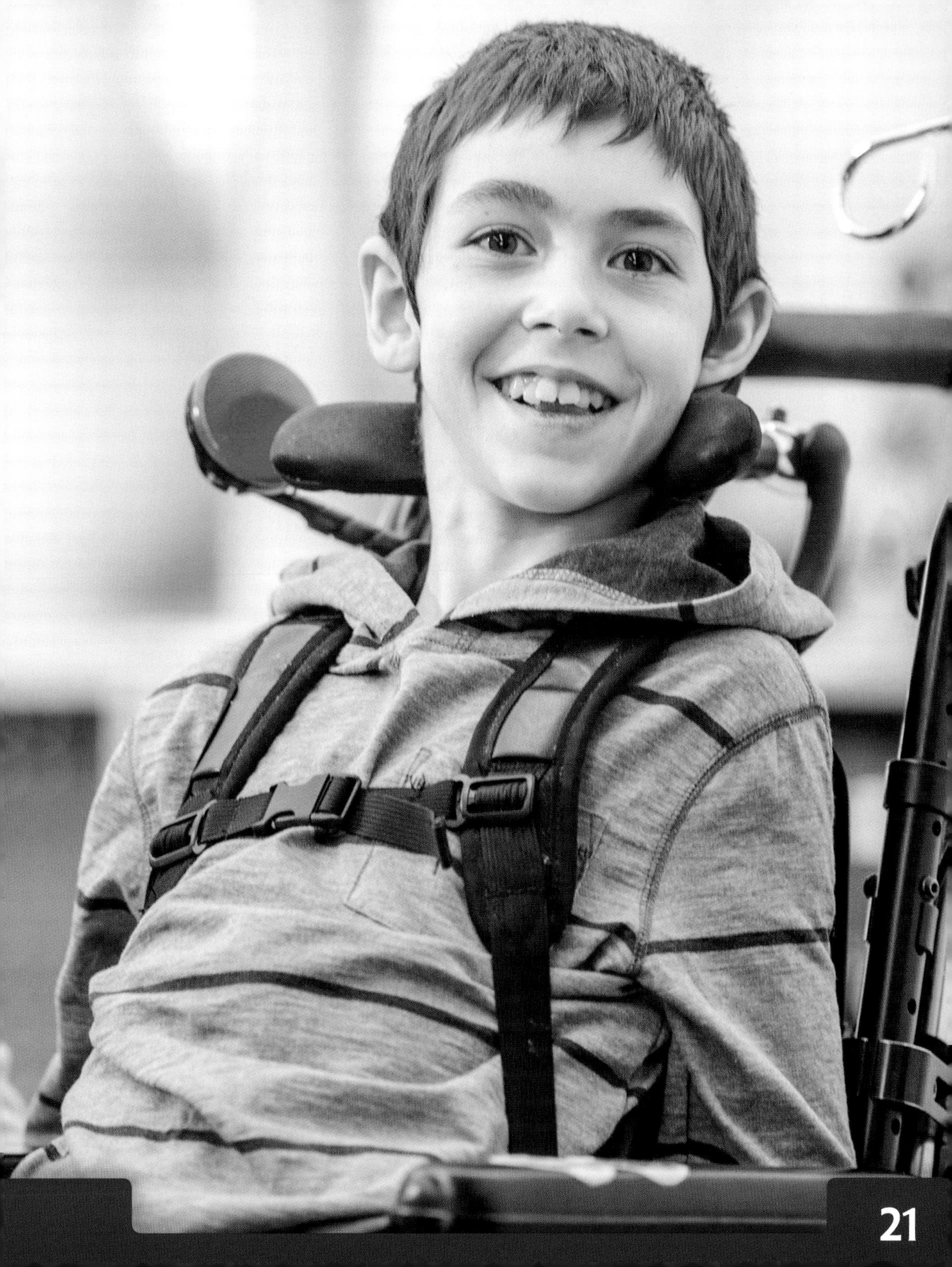

CHAPTER TEN

YOU'RE NOT ALONE

Stress can feel scary, but you're not alone. Everyone feels stressed at some point in their life. It's a completely natural feeling and part of being human. Stress can actually be a good thing sometimes.

Difficult and uncomfortable times can be opportunities for growth. When you learn to identify your stressors, you come to understand yourself better. When you come up with new ways to take care of yourself, you become stronger.

It's rare for people to reach a point where they feel completely calm and stress free. Instead of looking for ways to escape stress or hide from it, rest assured that next time you're stressed, you'll be ready to deal with it in a healthier way. You're strong enough to cope with stress and you're not alone!

GLOSSARY

acknowledge (ihk-NAAH-lihj) To show that something has been received or noticed.

attitude (AA-tuh-tood) A feeling or way of thinking that affects a person's behavior.

Buddhist (BOO-duhst) A person who studies Buddhism, which is a religion of eastern and central Asia based on the teachings of Guatama Buddha.

competitive (kuhm-PEH-tuh-tihv) Having a strong desire to win or be the best at something.

counselor (KOWN-suh-luhr) A person who gives advice.

develop (duh-VEHL-uhp) To bring out the possibilities of, to begin to have gradually, or to create over time.

focus (FOH-kuhs) To direct attention at something.

frustrated (fruh-STRAY-tuhd) Feeling angered or let down.

function (FUNK-shun) To work or operate.

intention (in-TENT-shun) An aim or plan.

irrational (ih-RAH-shuh-nuhl) Not based on reason.

meditate (MEH-duh-tayt) To spend time in quiet thought.

routine (roo-TEEN) A regular way of doing things in a particular order.

scenario (suh-NEHR-ee-oh) An account of a possible course of action or events.

INDEX

PRIMARY SOURCE LIST

Page 5
Fred Rogers on *Mister Rogers' Neighborhood* set. Photograph. Bettmann. November 24, 1976.

Page 17
Zen Buddhist monk leader Thich Nhat Hanh. Photograph. HOANG DINH NAM. April 20, 2007.

Page 18
Abraham Lincoln, three-quarter length portrait, seated, facing right. Photograph. Anthony Berger. February 9, 1864. Now kept at the Library of Congress Prints and Photographs Division, Washington, D.C.

WEBSITES

Due to the changing nature of Internet links, PowerKids Press has developed an online list of websites related to the subject of this book. This site is updated regularly. Please use this link to access the list: www.powerkidslinks.com/SSEL/calm